Dead Youth, or, The Leaks

ISBN: 978–1–933959–24–5

Cover design and typesetting: Mark Addison Smith
Collage: Ashley Lamb, *Fire Bucket*, 7 x 9-inches, mixed media, 2014

Litmus Press is a program of Ether Sea Projects, Inc., a 501(c)(3)
non-profit literature and arts organization. Dedicated to supporting
innovative, cross-genre writing, the press publishes the work of translators,
poets, and other writers, and organizes public events in their support.
We encourage interaction between poets and visual artists by featuring
contemporary artworks on the covers of our books. By actualizing the
potential linguistic, cultural, and political benefits of international literary
exchange, we aim to ensure that our poetic communities remain open-
minded and vital.

Litmus Press publications are made possible by the New York State
Council on the Arts with the support of Governor Andrew Cuomo and
the New York State Legislature. Additional support for Litmus Press
comes from the Leslie Scalapino–O Books Fund, individual members
and donors. All contributions are fully tax-deductible.

State of the Arts

NYSCA

Litmus Press   Small Press Distribution
925 Bergen Street #405   1341 Seventh Street
Brooklyn, New York 11238   Berkeley, California 94710
litmuspress.org   spdbooks.org

Library of Congress Cataloging-in-Publication Data
McSweeney, Joyelle, 1976–
  Dead youth, or, The leaks / Joyelle McSweeney.
    pages cm
  ISBN 978–1–933959–24–5 (pbk.)
  I. Title. II. Title: Leaks.
PS3613.C588D43 2014
812'.6—dc23
2014030926

Joyelle McSweeney

Dead Youth, or, The Leaks

a play in 4 acts

DRAMATIS PERSONAE

Prologue (Henrietta Lacks)
DEAD YOUTH (they are multiple and multiply)
Julian Assange
Abdi Wali Abdulqadir Muse
Antoine de Saint-Exupéry

Since all characters say their names repeatedly, physical resemblance of the actors to the historical personages to which these characters correspond, including apparent gender, racial, national or ethnic affiliation, is not required. The idea, rather, is to create an occult and unstable circuit of resemblances between events on the stage and events as they are distractedly remembered from 20th and 21st century 'history.' This play is an intentionally badly-wired allegory & enacts both less and more than allegory typically allows. It forgoes rational neatness and permits impossible events, jailbreaks from the Cartesian grid, political inflammation. In the mind of the audience, cast, crew or directors, the play may also call up certain ghosts currently absent from the main body of the play, such as Trayvon Martin, Chelsea Manning, the dead women of Juárez, *los desaparecidos*, etc. It is for this latter reason that the body of *DEAD YOUTH* is suggestively plural and flexing.

PROLOGUE

[PROLOGUE is a thirty-year-old African American woman dressed smartly in 1940's attire. She stands in a three-quarter pose and holds herself with dynamic, compact self-saturation.]

PROLOGUE: Hello I am your Prologue. Also known as Protégée.
My hair and blouse are neatly pressed,
my locks curled, as if 'dancing towards my face.'
My nails are short but red without a chip
and because I am a mother
I have to work in death as I did in life.
You will note I hoist a Petri dish, that's for illumination.
And an iPhone, that's for voyeurism.
And a tabloid, that's for tourism.
And a water bottle, that's for cash.
With the water, in my GI aspect,
I buy the hearts and minds of the local children
unless they slip under the wheels of the Humvee,
reaching for it.
Then they are rendered into the eternal ranks of
DEAD YOUTH
and join the dead insurgents and GI's.
DEAD YOUTH are the dark energy of this play.
They propagate a field in the void, an inverted Internet,
a compound interest that tugs information through
dark portals
chased by government men. In death they find no rest.
Decoy, decoy, and then...
Target Interface. They blow up again.

As the play begins, these DEAD YOUTH
[gestures to a spotlit clump of sleeping, tracksuited teens]
are all adrift on a disabled container ship
the MV Alabama Maersk, AKA Her Majesty's Infamy,
The Merchant of Venice, AKA the SS Smirk.
It has been oe'rmanned by three unlucky hijackers:
Julian Assange, blonde Internet villain, and two more

about to be revealed.
These men pursue their separate interests at first
unknown to each other.
And as the ranks of DEAD YOUTH are continually
added to
they swell the Smirk's corroded walls with baby
testosterone,
nylon jackets, hair cuts, body odor and antibodies.
If they do not dock soon, the cell will lyse.
The entire vessel will capsize.
This play is really about them.

Lord this lantern is HEAVY.
But it casts a clear black light.
That's the light the dead see
in their nightclub: the Dead Cat.
It's sharp as a stilletto.
It brings the secrets to light.
Guess what: we're living in a declivity
Called the twenty-first century.
None of us occupy a very terre haute now.
Every Sublime gotta have its rock bottom
every Mont Blanc its chasm
every blanc mange its spasm
every icy berg its lower berths.
To bear the damage.
That's me. That's thee, S.V.P.
I'm new here, to the twenty-first centuree, encargoed
with the fiji mermaids, hunger artists,
hottentott venuses, Jackson whites,
and those with the falling disease.
Oh My Anthropocene. My New Found Land.

Well, as they say, you can't choose your family,
Un coup de dés jamais n'abolira le hasard.
Our electric's been cut off.
Our ISP contract's been voided
Our satellite doesn't know us anymore.

We're steering upstream on Death's current
We are steering the ship
by starlight, on sheer infamy.
We are steering it with celerity, on sex drive, on instinct,
which means
we are steering it in a dream.
Close the shutters.
Take the marquee down. This Bates Motel
with its dead birds and killer boys inside
shall sail on,
marooned in night!

Did I mention my name is Henrietta Lacks?
All that you know about polio, space travel, most drugs,
how to make cells split in a fingerbowl forever
you know because I died a howling death
of cervical cancer in the colored ward
at Johns Hopkins, Baltimore, 1951.
When they autopsied me,
I wore a white nightgown of malignant pearls
inside my body, as if I were a Queen that had swallowed
my own crown
or a demented bride with her own cake sewn up inside.
Those bad cells went on doubling after my death
doubled and were sold off to labs and doubled again
suffered the rest of the twentieth cee without me
suffered spaced travel,
suffered bombs, made mice sick, wore makeup and
took drugs.
I was immortal in my ability to be knocked down
and spread myself out to take the punch again.
In this sense I am still a mother.
I am forever taking the punch in the gut.
No one asked for my consent.
And now the author of this play forces me
to stand up here and say these words:
Un coup de des jamais n'abolira
My body is this ship.

My body is this play
My body is gravity
rocking this ship
in the belly of the play
rocking this ship
in the belly of the play
the play rides inside of me
as a thought rides inside a thought
as a triply encrypted message in a junk envelope
dances around the Internet with unnatural suavity
it arrives on the inside of a second
& reveals a second to have an inside
a dark interstices made of undecidability.
—made out of me.
I have had to invent the whole world for you
once again from scratch:
rocking this ship
in the belly of the play
in the belly of the ship: flip flops, guns, "relief supplies."
in the belly of the play
a grifter, a pirate, a poser, DEAD YOUTH.
DEAD YOUTH are really the subject of this play.
Did I mention I am a mother?
Did I mention I am a mother?
A dead mother, a dead mother
A black electrick energy blooms from me.
I've smuggled it here from the twentieth cee.
Did I mention I am a mother?
I am. It's Mother's Day.
From now on I am the author of this play.

ACT ONE

*A bilious dawn above the SS Smirk. Two DEAD YOUTH
are strolling on deck. Others continue to clump like sneakered
lotus-eaters. White sneaker laces vine. The teens are crumpled
like lovely soiled money.*

Yellowish green money light.

DEAD YOUTH 1: How's the dawn?

DEAD YOUTH 2: Bilious. An ugly thing. So new, yet it glooms
    like cholangiocarcinoma. & glops its cellophane.

DEAD YOUTH 1: And how's the moon?

DEAD YOUTH 2: Green Cheese.

DEAD YOUTH 1: Yuk yuk

DEAD YOUTH 2: What is this, a school examination? Please.

DEAD YOUTH 1: What do I know about school? I breezed
    through that breezeway.

DEAD YOUTH 2: For me school was a breezey dream. Lit up with puff
    paint and smelly stickers. My friends, the girls, were
    budding cosmeticians…How they made a doll of me with
    the Sun-in and tweezers…Unfortunately I got dragged
    behind a three-wheeler at a post-prom party in the woods
    with a length of chain around my lissome neck. That was
    not such a friendly party as at first it seemed…

DEAD YOUTH 1: Dead to begin with. Dead as a painted moon
    upon a painted sea…

DEAD YOUTH 2: Oh, but I was dressed to the nines!

DEAD YOUTH 1: Then let's not get morose. I'm feeling good today. Some bug's got into my brain. Some kind of post-death inflammation is reanimating me. My circuits are firing like a firing squad. Repeating like a repeating rifle. I feel like I repeat my lines forever. Could finish school! Join the drum corps, dance team...

DEAD YOUTH 2: Junior ROTC!

DEAD YOUTH 1: Hustlers' Battalion.

DEAD YOUTH 2: Artists' Rifles.

DEAD YOUTH 1: CCTV! A special episode of Special Victims Unit.

DEAD YOUTH 2: O, we are a patriotic youth.

DEAD YOUTH 1: Today is a busy day. There are two press conferences, at noon.

DEAD YOUTH 2: Press conferences? And is there a press corps around here somewhere? A French Lick? A Coeur D'Alene?

DEAD YOUTH 1: Only us dead student bodies, as per usual. Also known as the Crumb Cohort, the Commingled Human Remains. But Mama Julian says we must keep up appearances. In case we are being surveilled with that green light with which they seek heat on pleasure boats, naughty things. Searching for leaks. For leaky youth. That leak from the throat. *[Bends his head back as from a nearly-severed neck]*

DEAD YOUTH 2: "They"?

DEAD YOUTH 1: The graduands of ROTC. Our past classmates. Our future campadres in the shadow army of DEAD YOUTH. AKA the Navy Seals.

DEAD YOUTH 2: Hmm. What fanciful names, these gangs today.
 Tho navy, what a flattering color...

DEAD YOUTH 1: Privacy is a chance operation. One must always
 have a poem ready in case the mic goes live.

DEAD YOUTH 2: When the cat's away / the lice do play.

DEAD YOUTH 1: I only regret that I have but one life to give—

DEAD YOUTH 2: —to the hive mind. Bury me standing

DEAD YOUTH 1: In the check-out line. I don't want to lose my place.

DEAD YOUTH 2: I'm double couponing.

DEAD YOUTH 1: I'm saving up for a doublewide.

DEAD YOUTH 2: That's why I joined the Navee!

DEAD YOUTH 1: That's why I R-O-T-C'd.

DEAD YOUTH 2: That's why I lost a hundred pounds so I could
 join the USMC.

DEAD YOUTH 1: I wanted to be a kindergarten teacher but
 couldn't afford the tuition. Then I got kidnapped and
 put on television...

DEAD YOUTH 2: "We don't take applications. Only
 commitments."

DEAD YOUTH 1: It's FUBAR. But YOLO. I'm AWOL. Lost at cee.

DEAD YOUTH 2: And now I'm in the gunsights for some mout
 breathing MP.

DEAD YOUTH 1: His itchy trigger-finger is hunga-ree for me.

DEAD YOUTH 2: Yum yum! Well when he finds you

BOTH: save some for me!

JULIAN ASSANGE: *[Entering, pushing a white cart full of beauty,
hygienic, and pharmaceutical supplies].* What's the buzz?
What's this I hear, bumblebees? Awake already? Like
the Internet, the sea's a casino, it keeps a clock not based
on human experience. Le-Roi-Soleil. No hours on the
see but the sun's hours. Shine and shine. That's my
motto, and that's the sun's. *[The DEAD YOUTH wake]*
Time for your morning treatment, sons. We blondes
cannot manage the raw light much longer. We must
have our morning ichor, our sun cream. Now, who can
tell me what IV's, hypos, bee-stings, and bone meal all
have in common.

DEAD YOUTH: They are all vectors!

JULIAN ASSANGE: That's right, geniuses. Of what?

DEAD YOUTH 1: Infections

DEAD YOUTH 2: Nutriment

DEAD YOUTH 3: Antigens

DEAD YOUTH 4: Information.

DEAD YOUTH 5: Everything but secrecy.

JULIAN ASSANGE: That's right. Secrecy is a landlocked ship. Like
that ship up on blocks in the Massif Central where Jean
Genet learned to be a sailor. Secrecy can't breathe. Privacy
is another matter. Privacy will find its subterranean
channel. Darkling privacy breathes like a sea. On privacy
we are a-drift. Tho lately, something is scripting us.
Something tugs.

DEAD YOUTH 1: Perhaps we've sprung a leak.

DEAD YOUTH 2: Perhaps our lymph is out of whack.

DEAD YOUTH 3: Perhaps we need a lumpectomy or

DEAD YOUTH 4: Federally funded mammogram or

DEAD YOUTH 5: Perhaps we've failed the smear test.

JULIAN ASSANGE: Enough. DEAD YOUTH, I adore you, and I have personally vouchsafed you here at my maternal bosom, even through I am a very hunted man. Mine may not be the very safest of bosoms in which to hide your lean, rodentine faces. As in the self-portraits of Frieda Kahlo, you may find yourself punctured from a number of difficult angles before the casual comedie is complete. Now, to continue the lesson: secrecy cannot move but information must. Because information is like air, mon amour, mon sacre coeur, and air hates vessels. A little air bubble in the vessel and the brain goes: stroke! But seamen love vessels and seminal vesicles and stroking and gossip contra secrecy. And we are seamen. At least temporarily.

DEAD YOUTH 1: Then what moves the ship?

DEAD YOUTH 2: And don't say 'love.'

OMNES DEAD YOUTH : AND DON'T SAY 'LOVE'!

JULIAN ASSANGE: I wouldn't dream of it. Our good ship, the SS Smirk, moves on dreams, and also because it is imbalanced. *[beat, worriedly, studies each of boys' faces]*. Some jerry-built wiring, some imbalance in the server load, is causing the ship to list. Then, something from the outside is pulling it off track...

DEAD YOUTH 3: A current?

JULIAN ASSANGE: A dream current, maybe… like a hot seam of toxic cells… a self-generating tumor… It's better than stagnation but, still, I am concerned. We are trackable when we move. We may be traced. That's why we must continually change our hairstyles.

DEAD YOUTH 2: Is it true, Julian, what my brother DEAD YOUTH tells me, that there will be two press conferences today?

DEAD YOUTH 1: Perhaps some military recruiter has gained access to the ship? Perhaps he wants us for a troop surge?

DEAD YOUTH 2: Some surge! More like a synth-track on loop.

DEAD YOUTH 1: More like a trackmark in a diseased forearm: suppurating. Skin coming loose.

ASSANGE: Ha, ha, DEAD YOUTH. Look at you, you're half corrupted, dear to me, but insipid as a flotilla of aspidistras in a locked office or an Easter Lily in June. You are waging no war the army wants, but I daresay you could mount one it doesn't! [twinkles] Still, I confess, I've heard that rumor myself, I heard you scratching in the skirtingboards last night, little rats, and it gnaws me like poison cheese…it drills me like a rotten tooth… I'm certainly not dressed for a duel, and I don't know who my second could be. This mystery raconteur's not one of you precocious corpses? With what did you signal the press? With your rancid grave-breath? By pressing the button in your knock-off Air Jordans, my Nikes of Samothrace, my croaked boy-dolphins of the River Styx? Phew, Dorothy! "There's no place like home. There's no zone like the canal zone."

DEAD YOUTH 2: Julian, have you stopped to wonder if there's someone else on this ship?

ASSANGE: Someone else on this ship? Well that would make for
a very ripe situation. A very ripe cheese indeed. This
ship's already as fetid as the team bus back to Belfast
after a track meet. That is, more fetid than any ship's
got a right to be.

DEAD YOUTH 3 & 4: I have an announcement. I had a vision in a
dream, a fragment.

DEAD YOUTH 1: Well, make it quick, that sun is getting high.

DEAD YOUTH 2: I'd like my portion of bone meal while we're waiting.

*[ASSANGE with eye dropper, hypo, IV goes around feeding
dead youth during the following speech. Other youth may foil
each other's hair]*

DEAD YOUTH 3: I was awake, all of a night.
I was awake, all through the night.
I think it's because it's my thirteenth birthday.
And also my aniversaree.

DEAD YOUTH 1: He means of the day he died.

DEAD YOUTH 3: And also my aniversaree.
Of the night they wrapped the barbed wire around me
and threw me into the river.
I was chained to a cash register.
Forever. Legal tender.
So I could purchase knowledge.
So I could chase after knowledge forever
In the madrassa of the muddy river
and never come up again.
Eli eli Allah Allah
How the river broke my teeth
forced its knowledge into me
gave up all its information
hammered it into my brainstem

O I knew everything then
at last and for the last time
I was smarter than a pentium chip
smarter than a flash drive
the moment I died

DEAD YOUTH 2: This one thinks he's a visionary.

DEAD YOUTH 4: And also it was my anniversaree
So I was also walking the deck last night
Reliving my handful of memories…
O on the night I died
I had been up that night coding
I had been up all night coding coding
On the night I died on the night I died
That was the night before the day we'd go live
But 'we' never did go live
I deleted I from we
I permanently destroyed the encryption keys
The day before the night I died
And all that death caught up with me
I had to go meet it in the closet
I had to go meet the knot
I couldn't beat it so I soldered
like a soldier off the base
I had to go meet it with a tie wrapped round my throat
I had to meet it with a bag over my face

DEAD YOUTH ONE: And this one's an entrepreneur.

DEAD THREE AND FOUR: We had to go meet it on the deck last night
We could not sleep, our anniversaree
Kept rising in us like a moon or a rumor
We had to go meet it on the deck
We strolled like a couple of lady journos
Circling the globe to rapturous applause
Telegraphing back to rival papers
Our arrivals in split skirts and dusters

O, that anniversary kept compelling us 'round the deck!
Like a couple of planets or a couple of clockhands
Diminutive, dwarf things that could wreck no orbits
We circled, clasped hands, and moaned.
Then with our eyes we did espy
With the aid of our steamy lorgnettes
A rubber craft sidle up to the vessel
And a young man scale the Smirk walls!
It was a young man, as beautiful as the night
With beautiful teeth like the cancerous growths
Enpearling hot organs en la crevasse de l'autopsie
O his smile irradiated our dirty gazes
And his dark suit flapped around him like a piece of night
But was a piece of nylon, for it had that signature bark
So we knew him for a teen
And he climbed and he climbed the ladder
rung after rung, rung after rung
he climbed the sheer flank of the vessel
when he arrived at deck-level
our vision failed; we think he disappeared into some coil.

JULIAN ASSANGE: Youth, this is indeed a vision.

YOUTHS 3 and 4: But that is not all, that is not all.
No sooner had the dark-clad teen
disappeared into the vessel,
than another figure arose on the opposite flank.
All clad in white, neither man nor woman.
In a crisp uniform that did not flap
and a hat like a piece of new moon concentrate.
And climbed up the opposite flank, the opposite flank
And disappeared likewise in the bowels of the ship.

JULIAN ASSANGE: Youth, this double vision is full of fancy.

OMNES DEAD YOUTH: Yes full of fancy, full of the night.

JULIAN ASSANGE: I fear it like fancy, I fear it like the night.

OMNES DEAD YOUTH: I fear it like fancy, I fear it like the night.

JULIAN ASSANGE: Youth, I do not know what
        mad double agency joins us.
        What doppelganger, what devil a deux
        What mad double thought, what one and what zero
        does not equal two,
        Which antigen, which antidote. But I do know
        that I must speed up my preparations for my press
        conference.
        I will deliver my address as a means of securing
        my hold on the plot
        and thus hastening us to our destination
        which I shall reveal so shortly, but which for now I hold
        to my breast, a secret,
        as I hold you, dear children.
        While I ready myself, please perform the short masque
        we have rehearsed. *[exits]*

DEAD YOUTH 1: *[to audience]* Ladies and gentlemen,
        may we perform for you
        An act of infamy:
        a video leaked by Private Bradley Manning (allegedly!)
        and published to the world by Julian Assange on the
        website, Wikileaks. It took a borrowed supercomputer
        to decrypt this information. It took the hiviest of hive
        minds. You will note it is green like any act that grows
        in the dark of the crypt. You will note it lives.
        Ladies and gelignites
        Collateral Murder!

        *[For this short night ballet, the light on the stage shifts to suggest
        night vision. The DEAD YOUTH shroud themselves in black
        robes like burkas. The vision should be grainy like radioactive
        grains; action should leave green lines on the air like vines in
        the work of Aubrey Beardsley. A portion of the audio to the
        famous 'Collateral Murder' video should play, while the DEAD
        YOUTH play the part of the bodies in the videos, walking,*

taking shelter, being shot, arriving in the van, being shot,
being pulled into the van, being shot. The DEAD YOUTH
do the DEATH DROP. The figures of the DEAD YOUTH
should almost seem to be 'recycled'—shot and revived and
reentering the stream of violence represented in the video. For
a fancy special effect, the video may appear to 'rewind,' 'loop,'
or 'repeat.' Such DJ effects are up to the company.]

DEAD YOUTH 1: *[removing his burka, wiping away sweat]* Phew!
What an atrocity.

DEAD YOUTH 2: What a day at the races.

DEAD YOUTH 1: It's hard work, this afterlife.

DEAD YOUTH 2: It's hard work, being a teen-corpse on the SS Smirk
sailing for who-knows-where with the blond assassin,
Julian Assange.

PROLOGUE: *[entering stage. Gravely.]* Yea, verily. What an atrocity.
What an atrocity. What an atrocious leak.
O it leaks a bilious green that carries black matter with it.
O it leaks all over the screen.
O it is all too recognizable, the grief of mothers.
O it is like acid poured on the face of the Internet
O it turns all flesh to fluid so that it might leak
O it runs ideas together
Brain fluid flusters in the nose
Of the schoolgirl, of the pharaoh.
The DEAD YOUTH are all dressed as mothers
in this scene.
O it might bring on a vengeance.
O it might bring on a spell of vengeance.
O it might draw a violence to the scene.
O it must, maybe it must!
O watching face. O humanitee.
You like to ape the moon. Peel your face back
to the skull. At the seat of the skull: the teeth.

That vicious jewelry
wears a merchant's grin. As it peruses the wares.
It always wears that same bare face.
Vanity, vanity,
The mind is media
for a life of crime
but wants to pretend otherwise. That's what
the leak divines.
It taps the flux and drains the pus from the line.
Where it will live on into infinitee
on the Internet. Take it from me.
Mother of a very immortal line.
My cells live on in culture in their malignancy.
I'm dead so I can live two places: everywhere
and on the Internet.
Only malignant cells can divide like that
i.e. unto infinitee. That's the bottom line.
And I'm the heavy-weight champeen.
And that's atrocitee.

ACT TWO

JULIAN ASSANGE: *[He is dressed in a grey suit. His shining hair is clean and feminine and light-bearing as a shampoo ad. Lucifer hair! He stands at a podium as at a press conference. He addresses the audience. The DEAD YOUTH pose, swoon, smirk, stand at attention, variously]*

Hello my name is Julian Assange.
Thank you for your attention to those burka'd teens.
They are in a work-study program.
They are studying abroad.
They are in juvenile detention.
They are receiving extra-credit.
They are part of a good will exchange between our
two nations.
They are on a chain-gang.
They are all out on work-release.
Though DEAD, they are studying for their GED's.
& degrees in dance therapy.

I would like to deliver my prepared remarks.
But I am distracted by these teens.
They are members of a dance team.
They are on their way to an abstinence convention.
They are drinking absinthe.
They are aspiring drone pilots.
They are on their way to an interfaith prayer breakfast.
They shot two convenience store clerks for one
hundred dollars.
Their van has crashed, and they are walking along
the highway.
If they do not find gas soon, they will have to eat
the weakest one.
They are going completely feral just a few miles
from the highway,
listening to death metal, practicing magick.
They are running pornographic services out of

their bedrooms.
They are at soccer practice.
They work in their uncle's convenience store at night.
They do their algebra homework.
They study war.
They are boy soldiers, hustlers, 'knock-off jihadi.'
They invented Facebook.
They are entrepreneurs and visionaries.
X-game competitors, budding baristas,
junior rapists, virgin martyrs and walking delinquencies.
They are beauties and atrocities.
I can't stop looking at them.
They could not survive what was required of them.

I will now deliver my prepared remarks.
Prepared for me by the Author of the feast, which is
a cell line, or Fate.
The Smirk is full of noises. *[returns to teens]* The isle
is full of teens.
I'm bundling up packets of information
in strong ribands of junk for its own protection
and tossing it into the sea. Perhaps you've seen *The Tempest.*
Perhaps you know how this ends. Some things sink,
while other things float.
Others are enraptured in a tree.
We call this plot.
And tho I am a well known evangeline for privacy
I'm no angel. More like an ancient greek.
I like to lift the cloak off a diplomatic channel to watch
the current phreak!
I love privacee. I love transparancee.

DEAD YOUTH: Except!

ASSANGE: *[continuing]* I love secret identitees. I am mixed on the
          subject of redaction.
          I am a leftist.
          I don't hate the state

DEAD YOUTH: Except!

ASSANGE: *[continuing]* I believe emperors should be naked.
      O complexitee!
      Here's a riddle for you to work out, O lightening bugs,
      paparazzi: abominable
      secrecy, delectable privacy, holee transparencee,
      cursed detectibility, desired accountability...
      Like: alive or dead in the box, what is the cat thinking.
      That box is the Internet. One cat brain cell is the leaker.
      Another brain cell is the leak-receiver.
      The nearest synapse is the battle creek.
      But the leak doesn't cross there
      it jumps all over the brain
      lighting up every synapse
      in a total war. A grand mal!
      till noone knows where it is going or where it has been.
      O device maudit! O seizure!
      O brain on work release
      from the regime of cause and effect.
      Eventually it reaches its destination, me,
      I publish it on Wikileaks
      and that's an end.
      Game over, kitty-kat. Zap. zap.

      O Wikileaks. Nymph-stage, perfect gesture at the
      perfect time in the minute lifecycle of a dayfly, which
      has to die at day's end, lump it or leave it, leak or limp.
      I wanted to build on you but who can build on lymph.
      Our mistake was to publish the leaks ourselves, not
      just ship them to some other destination. We were left
      holding the bag with the cat out. Became the chopping
      block, target practice. We were happy to take the blows
      from those conquistador's arquebusses and blunder-
      busses, really we were, but when the banksters and
      credit card companies blocked our pipeline of donations,
      that was really an end. Wikileaks! I swear to revive you
      once I reach my destination with the help of these

fun-loving DEAD YOUTH.

Uhm, I'd like to introduce DEAD YOUTH, and
thereby a portion of the plot:

OMNES DEAD YOUTH: *[this rap accompanied by a rhythmic dance. The*
YOUTH may trade verses and sing some portions in unison]
Hello I'm Dead Youth
also known as a lion at the Baghdad Zoo
airvacked to Stockholm there I went symptomatic
comatic asthmatic astigmatic
but in my distress
I DID perfect the hologram kick
Like Zlatan Junior Imbrohimovich
But when soldiers filled the stadium
with their carbines, biceps and rank nasturtiums
I was laid out on the pitch
Dead, I fled to a dream Zurich
Where I died again of insight.
I padded on gold paws
lived on in the svelte vaults, read the golden
embossments
memorized the serial numbers
my brain better than a supercomputer
I maintained like a mainframe
but more better splendor
still you can't live on love. Well, not 4-ever.
Hello so I'm dead again some bored john killed me,
some bulldozer. A falling wall. A body bomb
Answering its phone, a days work at the dump
Pulling the laptop apart for its metals.
Playing an extra in an international Ponzi scheme
cum-Gotterdammerung. I was a mule or camel.
The deal gone bad, I was hung
from the overpass headless with a name carved on my chest
Each time I came back from the dead
now I'm dead and my knowledge too
Unless Julian Assange can quickly speed me to a port

to reboot. Till then I'm just idling here on the deck
tho I was heading for Art's shores.

JULIAN ASSANGE: *[resuming fondly]* O Art! That destination's too
lofty. I have another one in mind…
In farthest Queensland, my colonie,
Magnetic Island, named for a mythical sleeping force
that made Captain Cook's cock, uhm, compass leap
up like robin
directing him for the shore,
indetectible evermore. That black allure
could shock all the new Sony AM dreammachines,
crack safes, forge canvasses, eat the code off
any barnacled bit of credit card strip or VHS cassette…
I lived there in a lean-to, as my mother
lived in bikinis. Later we moved to the shelter
on the mainland
for battered moms and teens, she bought me
a Commodore 64
on credit, because she loved me, we lived like a
battery hens
on chips, I peck-pecked our 8-bits. Lean times.
Dear mother.
On our notorious hair
we brushed a deleterious dye
called Invisiblonde. Called Slender Prey's
Intoxicating Hide.

ASSANGE and DEAD YOUTH: My mother JonBenet and me
My mother Margaret Thatcher.
My mother Henrietta Lacks.
My mother Antigone.
My mother strong correlation
Palingenesis, telomarese,
recapitulation
My mother twentieth cee
My mother enceinte
My mother epicene

My mother in surburbia
My mother sleeper cell
My mother human error
yellow cake or Zyklon B
My mother migrating heron
that, chopped up in the engine,
brings down the corporate jet
My mother trashed reputation
My mother Hitchcock blonde
My mother windswept highlands
My mother updo
My mother bog
My mother bared midriff, dirndl, sari,
sandal, buckskin, wristwatch, hijab,
Who survived my birth
but barely
Whose idea of groceries
was a bottle of bleach or pills
a donation to the church or the Panthers
lived in a vat of spaghetti
died in a petri dish
My mother in Arcadia ego
My mother botulinum in hypo
wiped toilets
in gloves and smock
played bridge in
evening dress
sabotaged the trainbridge
shot up the bank vault
worked the third shift
was throttled in halter top
was choked in a stalking
was brought up on charges
Became a rogue signatory
No longer agreed to the plot
Divested of media resources
became a relentless top
and crashed the last century's banquet

a radioactive
grain in every dish
Her name was Estrogena,
Aspartame, Nicotiana,
Thalidomida, Saccharina,
Carcinoma, Sacerdota,
Carmen,
Carcinogen…

JULIAN ASSANGE: *[patting the shoulder of DEAD YOUTH, calming
them, distributing pills, talking a kind of soothing patter].*

Hello, I am Julian Assange, I've been assassinated by
my mother.
My mother was divine. A divine assassination.
She edited and improved me.
She shot me full of gold.
Protected me, gilt me, guided me, hid me, and
bought me a Commodore 64
Now I endeavor to be a golden like my mother
to radiate hot pixels of information
to cell-divide forever
to stage a pussy riot, to offer teens of all nations
hot gobblets of information
pus-gold and liberating, the rays of my inflammation.
These pets you see gathered around me are little runts
I've collected from the NICU ward in Memorial
Hospital in South Bend
Indiana. Poor things were born
addicted to oxycodone, oxycontin, valium and other
narcotics.
Born like princesses with lotus feet. Only things fit
them are Nikes and IV's. Poor things are asleep.
I had to save them from the cuddler army of 54
retiree church organists, an invasive species.
I carry in this box a little code to feed them on.
sorry a little comb, they're bees.
Please help yourself before helping others, little

species little protégées. It's on demand!
It's all you can eat on repeat forever.
in the event of two similar die-offs, the greater
of two die-offs is still similar. Infinity resembles
infinity to the dead.
That's why they need a mom like me
and how I can be one: resemblance
is a magick power. I copy my mother
& live here in drag like a mortal.
I just don't have a normal mortal motor.
I'm an abnormal mater!
Abnormal matter!
But unlike cancer, I have a motive.
It's to keep these teens alive on the Internet.
I feed them like roses, I feed them privacee.
My motive is indetectible to you
because you don't want to see it.
But my moralitee is a rare and strong growth.
It configures a colonee.
It grows in night vision.
It thrives on unnatural light.

ABDI WALI ABDULQADIR MUSE: Assange, I have arrived.

ASSANGE AND OMNES DEAD YOUTH: *[with extreme courtliness and
        pleasure]* HOW NOW DEAD YOUTH!

MUSE: Although I am a teen I am not dead. I have come to
        occupy this ship. I need it.

ASSANGE: To occupy this ship? Faddish lad. Despite my suit, do
        we resemble a corporation? Is it Bring- Your-DEAD-
        YOUTH-to-Work Day?

MUSE: ASSANGE, I am a desperate man. In just a few hours, they
        are shipping me to Terre Haute.

ASSANGE: Handsome Youth, albeit not dead: you are welcome to

join us on our ad-hoc journey, our ragtag army of
questionable devices. But if you wish to steer this vessel
anywhere but Magnetic Island, I suggest you find
another means of transportation. Allow me to quote
from Mayakovsky's dead letter: this boat has smashed
upon the rocks of 'byt'. I.E., the Smirk is listing badly.
We stole it from from a shippy sick bay where they were
going to ravage it for parts. I mean salvage it. But now it
is our salvation, albeit limited. It is following a mystery
current, lately detected, a smooth seam. It only goes one
way. And that way, if I may be so blunt, is my way.

MUSE: Assange, allow me to reassure you. My capture of the site
will last but an interval. I have urgent business to attend
to. I know it is my fate to be entirely landlocked and
sealed away from the Internet till my fiftieth birthday.

OMNES: GASP!

MUSE: I was sentenced this morning in a New York court. OH,
is any fate worse than Terre Haute, Indiana? And I speak
as one brought up in 'war-torn Somalia'! Tomorrow I will
be flown out in chains under armed escort. There I will
take up residency with bungler jihadist and the back-
up director of the Gambino crime family. It is rather
glamorous company for one such as me, who only left
his mother's side two weeks ago.

OMNES DEAD YOUTH: Two weeks?!

DEAD YOUTH 5: I also died two weeks ago.
I haven't yet adjusted. Mama Julian says
I'm adjusting poorly. I may have an adjustment disorder.
I may cause a small but crucial aberration in the field
with my level of maladjustment.
I could sink the ship
before we reach Magnetic Island
or even start an island of my own, helas,

a cancer cluster.
He's wrapped me in a lead apron
And kept me away from important instruments.
My story goes:
A drone hit me.
Nosed me out with its nosecone.
Zeroed me out of the Anthropocene.
Although I was, like the drone, an American.
It pushed a wall on me. It made a date with me!
O dinner date! O pederastic drone!.
These DEAD YOUTH call me 'Barack' but I don't like it.
I am a teen who died eating dinner with my cousin
and that's all. It was not a happy fate. *[fights tears]*

MUSE: *[placing hand on DEAD YOUTH 5's shoulder]* My sympathies
　　　are with you, Abdulrahman. But you've got to buck up.
　　　This is the new situation!

DEAD YOUTH 5: O God, God! *[burying his face in Muse's shoulder]*

DEAD YOUTH 1: *[exasperated]* O, weep weep!

DEAD YOUTH 2: O gag. It's alien corn hour.

ASSANGE: Intriguing Somalian youth, I know your country well
　　　from the Internet. I think of it fondly for it figured in
　　　several of our earliest leak-tests. Then our 'Cablegate'
　　　revealed the US government dipping its big toe in the
　　　riptide of your perpetual war.

MUSE: I hope not perpetual.

ASSANGE: Well one can hope. Malignancy has a way of sticking
　　　around in the system. It mounts the lymph nodes like an
　　　Internet and rides. It opens a franchise. You may have
　　　concluded this during the handful of years you have
　　　endured in the Anthropocene.

MUSE: ASSANGE and YOUTH, I have no time to waste.
          Please allow me to begin again.
          I'm Abdi Wali Abdulqadir Muse.
          Though I have many names and synonyms
          Approxi-nyms and acronyms
          Provided for me by journalists and the Internet.
          The Internet, my second mother. *[All nod, approvingly]*
          I come from Galka'yo, Somalia, what's known
          as a divided city
          due to a continuously collapsing state
          a conflict which expands according to no known
          galactic models
          continually making more of itself according to local tastes
          and outside interference, as you referenced in your
          'Cablegate'
          I am 16, 17, 19, and 26, also over 18
          according to American authorities, paving the way for
          prosecution.
          I am between 16 and 17 according to my mother
          continuously phoning from Galka'yo.
          According to she, I was
          "coaxed into piracy by gangsters with money."
          and have been gone just two weeks.
          That is my prologue, and what's left of it
          is immediately going past
          and folding up into a vanishing point
          according to hegemony's impossible CGI,
          its skill with dispossession—
          But what is this? I hear someone approaching!
          I hear someone muttering, clattering
          the loud clang of a too-long saber knocking against a
          polished boot!
          A visor knocking the bridge of a sweating nose
          as if some inept knight were climbing up a ladder!
          O who is approaching? O is it Authoritee?
          Can it be I am detected? O, ASSANGE, am I slain?
          [he scrambles to hide].

ANTOINE DE SAINT-EXUPÉRY: *[a pilot. enters with bluster and saber*
rattles. He steps up the podium previously occupied by
ASSANGE and delivers this address, haughtily]

Hello I'm Antoine de Saint-Exupéry author of Le Petit
Prince. I am the beloved aviateur-auteur-and-homme-
du-lettres-francais. I died in 1944, mort por la France.
Being dead, I can board this ship without disturbance.
Monsieur Assange has arranged the security that way,
doomed liberal. It's hardly sea-worthy. It's hardly air-
tight. Ah, but all errors are human errors when it comes
to privacee. To begin: I am the dream interloper, I am
the white hunter and these assorted perverts are the
prey. I am played by a woman. Like many women
associated with aviation, I have disappeared: myself,
Howard Hughes, Lindbergh's baby. Since your pre-
monition, have you ship-rats run a search? Have you
thought about draining the loch? Have you thought
about dredging the apartment complex? Have you
thought about going door-to-door? Erica Pratt, seven-
years-old of Philadelphia, freed herself from a kidnapper
by chewing through duct tape and escaping through a
broken basement window. In an article on the Internet,
the police chief glowingly notes, "she's suffered NO
HARM WHATSOEVER!" Yet this vessel, the Merchant
Vessel MAERSK Alabama, AKA the SS Smirk, on the
other hand, which I am here to inspect, and, let's face it,
confiscate, cannot effect an escape. It's listing, it's riding
a sludgy margin. Something stinks. For one thing, is
that Julian Assange, or just another pirate, or both? I
insist as a Frenchman stroking my kepi, this ship's
forms aren't in order. Her manifest ain't blest. This
blonde might be a stowaway, some homeless mom
leaving the night shift at Dunkin Donuts with a packet
of reject munchkins for her litter kids. I might look
like Claude Reins from Casablanca, flaky as a pastry,
my coiffeur a vol-au-vont cushion for my kepi, a cravat
spoiling for an honorary cross, but as a woman, I'm the

endgame, I'm the belle dame san merci, bon homies,
I'm a swallow, a tough cookie that lays its radioactive
grains in the throat, and I say, she's leaky, this blonde,
and this tub, The SS SMIRK. Her story don't hold
water. It don't hold up. Listen up, paparazzi, papyrus,
inamorati, dead and sleazee guests. These papers are
thin as leaves, they show a ghost cargo, ghost crew.
[beat] Unfortunately I can only read these ghost papers
because I, too, am dead. I keep radioing ship-to-shore
on my magic instrument but I can't get through on
pre-war knowledge. It's just birdscratch, birdsong: Who
dunit who dunit To who. To who. I'm dead to them like
last century's flu. I'm going to have to bring this vessel
under my own command with no help from outside
intermediaries. AND there's no telling what's in that
box he's fingering. Could be a dirty bomb!

JULIAN ASSANGE: It's an organ.
It's for shipboard services.
And I'm a missionary / mercenary.
All above board.

DEAD YOUTH: *[prankishly]* buzz buzz

ASSANGE: OK It's it's a crate of oranges.
They're alive with fruit flies, all indentured workers
with their vaccines and their papers from Monsanto.
All above board.

DEAD YOUTH: buzz buzz

ASSANGE: OK It's a miniature server farm.

DEAD YOUTH: Buzz!

ASSANGE: Its video game controllers
a junked prototype of the Wii

DEAD YOUTH: Weeeee!!

ASSANGE: I'm taking them to Vaguest Africa
        for starving children to use
        in the camp for refugees.
        To keep fit and practice drone warfare
        in case they are adopted by Americans in the future.
        Mine's a mission of relief!!

DEAD YOUTH: *[like a saxophone]* BUZZ!

ASSANGE: Ok it's bees.

ANTOINE DE SAINT-EXUPÉRY: Sir you won't use that tone with me. I
        represent the internecine interests of France, Lower
        Saxony, and American shipping lines. I am the universal
        solvent and when I move my bowels it's like a gold
        mine. Ok? I'm throwing my weight around, skinny.
        Now, I want to talk to a grown up.

ALL: That's me!

MUSE: *[emerging from his hiding place]* Ahem, that's me. Monsieur,
        may I be at your service?

ANTOINE DE SAINT EXUPÉRY: Who're you?

MUSE: My name is Abdi Wali Abdulqadir Muse. I am a valet of
        that man there. As you can see I'm black.

ANTOINE DE SAINT EXUPÉRY: And why isn't he talking to me directly?

ABDI WALI ABDULQADIR MUSE: Sir we are all white men here. That is,
        in that, we believe in the rule of law, trickle down
        economics, the chain of command, cheap clothing and
        container ships. A chain that on the one hand moves the
        goods, and on the other holds me here in my place, you
        in yours.

ANTOINE DE SAINT EXUPÉRY: Fiend, you can reason.

ABDI WALI ABDULQADIR MUSE: Good sir, I am no fiend but a valet, in
    a job-training program, what your brother Briton would
    call a 'training scheme'. I hope to return to my own land
    and open up a school for valets. We will teach subservience
    without the malfeasance, the smile without the guile.
    How to wipe the white crumbs from the table with a
    knife. A blunt instrument. It may sound out of date to
    you but some things never go out of style. Par example,
    did you hear the new Obama Administration 'e-verify'
    immigration labor bill includes a footnote exempting
    "footmen" from requiring documentation checks?

ANTOINE DE SAINT EXUPÉRY: That sounds to me like so much tropic
    hyperbole. For 'tropic' read 'sophist', NB.

ABDI WALI ABDULQADIR MUSE: Not at all, sir. Settle into this wingchair.
    Let me and these rank lads, my pupils, perform the very
    law for thee.

ANTOINE DE SAINT EXUPÉRY: Your pupils? I got the distinct impression
    these kids were with the blonde!

    *[ABDI WALI ABDULQADIR MUSE tut tuts
    ANTOINE's objections and sweeps him into a fatherly wing-
    chair. ASSANGE, MUSE, and DEAD YOUTH perform
    COLLATERAL MURDER TWO. Here the burkas return
    and the DEAD YOUTH with MUSE perform another
    excerpt of the famous video according to the strictures above]*

ASSANGE: O lovely, lovely. DEAD YOUTH you are so talented,
    so flexible and double jointed, so committed in your
    willingness to become any kind of media. It was just like
    watching a revolutionary mural or frieze, both analogue
    and digital. How it counted itself off. How it moved in
    frames, and how those frames moved. O I'm willing to
    run interference for you children from here to Infinitee—

or, preferably, Magnetic Island. That's just the kind of
mom I am. A blonde one. Hum! And you must under-
stand, villainous Exupéry, that this performance is both
a literal depiction and a kind of allegory for all kinds of
less visible violences which are an intrinsic part of our
cultural fabric but hidden inside diplomatic cables or
mental black sites. You see it here, but it's happening
there. DEAD YOUTH will bring it to light!

EXUPÉRY: Oh that was a marvelous play. It had a certain native
simplicity, a native joy, an interest in aping and imitation,
but at the same time Very European, very martial, very
involved in divisions and counting and perfect rule
of law with plenty of exemptions and exemptions and
indications and—

Hey! What is the meaning of this! I am strapped to my
chair and cannot move and liberate myself?! Is this a
kidnapping? O! Removed from history by some rank
plot! I am full of rue! O Mama said this would happen
if I didn't keep my feet on the ground! Just like Patty
Hearst and Amelia Earhart! She was not such a mama
as you *[he nods at Assange]*.

MUSE: I thank you not to abuse Monsieur Julian. He's been a
bit of a prick but is now rehabilitating himself as a
mother and teaching these homeless dead children to
rehab junk ships and hack into computer systems. It's
basically Schindler's wrist. Now, what did you think of
the play?

EXUPÉRY: What did I think of it? I admit, I enjoyed it, at first
blush, with the carefree jouissance as a schoolboy which
is universally prized and protected, even on this ques-
tionable vessel, which I am beginning to regret I every
mounted, this Puke Parnassus.

ABDI WALI ABDULQADIR MUSE: Behave like a gentleman, sir. That's

enough of your lingua franca. Ah, mother tongue
can be such a dick in a throat, such a svarte garrote!
Of course, as one whore said to the other, "There is
no mother tongue. Only a power takeover by a
dominant language."

EXUPÉRY: For a ship full of 'mothers', I find your deportment lacks
tenderness.

ABDI WALI ABDULQADIR MUSE: Lacks tendernesse! Sir, since you are a
master of these things, let me ask you: what is the most
tender thing of all?

EXUPÉRY: A new mother.

ABDI WALI ABDULQADIR MUSE: Well we've got that, if you'll excuse
the expressions, in spades. We've got Monsieur Assange.
However, this discussion is becoming circular, like a
chapeau, a case of crabs in a seminary or a firing squad.
Let me tell you a little story. I saw this on Al Jazeera.
There is a disease called Chagas disease common among
the rural poor of Latin America. In Argentina, for
example, the poor share their small homes with a tiny
irritating insect called the vinchuca. It bites these poor
peasants as they sleep. It sips their blood, it shits or
vomits a little bit of this blood back into their blood-
stream. As it does, it also releases a microscopic parasite,
the flagellate protozoan Trypanosoma cruzi. In photo-
micrographs, this protozoan looks as slender and harm-
less as a little girl's hair riband or a streamer from a bike.
But in the body of a peasant, toxin runs all through
the body, causes celldeath, including in the heart. Now
the peasant man can no longer swing his axe. And why
must he swing his axe? Because that is his livelihood: he
makes axe handles. The tessellating pattern of subsistence
labor snags and staggers. The axe is swung but poorly.
The mother now swings the axe, now the children, and
now noone. My parable is concluded.

EXUPÉRY: That's a parable? I don't follow.

ABDI WALI ABDULQADIR MUSE: Allow me to quote another great
        author, Mr. Herman Melville: FOLLOW YOUR
        LEADER. *[smacks him]* Sir, you are slower than these
        dead youth. Perhaps your kepi is too tight. I am here
        to read my rights into the record. I'm here for my
        MIRANDA rights! That is, I'm here because I love
        the Brave New World despite the people in it. I like
        Assange and his mooncalfs, the DEAD YOUTH. So
        let me begin again. As a human inmate on earth in the
        year 2013, I have been bitten by many things. That is,
        I have been subjected to many things, mostly against
        my will. To the point that will itself seems to be a
        poison and not the same for every man. The whole
        body of Somalia, par example, if we agree that it exists,
        has been swathed in a garment of toxic and nuclear
        waste for some decades now thanks to the depravity
        of wealthier nations and global shipping companies.
        We've been too embroiled in a convenient civil war to
        defend her. The Indian Ocean tsunami revealed the
        whole plot, brought huge barrels of oozing to nuclear
        and hospital waste to our shores and wiped it as salves
        into the RNA of my brethren. Now, some among us
        have styled ourselves shepherds of the sea, gone out to
        garner a sort of immediate reparation for these system-
        ic damages from passing ships in the form of ransoms.
        Others among us, admittedly, have been motivated by
        baser things, such as the desire to eat. Which one right
        now, ask yourself, would you rather I be, a man moti-
        vated by justice, or a man who wants something to eat?

[beat, beat]

What about a man who wants to eat justice?
And what would such a man shit out into
Justice's bloodstream?
And this, then, cher aviateur, my dirty chevre,

my cabriolet, is the meaning of my parable.
So many things I have been made to eat. So
many little things have eaten me.
I will learn from that. Let me be unto this
world the bacterium
pinkly slender as a girl's riband
that eats and changes hearts
until the muscle of the great man falters
no axe can swing
and no blow can fall

EXUPÉRY: O pirate! I am slain.

ABDI WALI ABDULQADIR MUSE: When I hear grown men use this term
'pirate,' I reach for my gun. It seems it only applies to
me and a pack of shut-in dead and down-market teens.

OMNES DEAD YOUTH: *[happily]* We're going to need a bigger boat!'

MUSE: We're going to need a bigger gun. Somehow we're the
scourge, the pirates, and not the credit default swappers,
stock traders, nation crashers, corporate raiders, pharma-
ceutical hockers, civil war fomenters, forest burners,
contractors, mercenaries, military recruiters, plant
closers or anyone else who bleeds 'the system' for all its
milky staph while leaving behind a crumpled stalk that
is good for nothing but releasing toxic compounds as it
breaks down. It seems that only I, who have nothing, not
even a functioning country, I who rationally recognize
what's right in front of my face, that the exchange value
of a single white man's life is without limit, that the
cargo of a single boat of cheap junk, crude, or even
waste headed to port is far greater than all the souls in
my war-wracked region, should be condemned for my
savagery, my wild-eyed 'rapacity'? Sorry, if I'm 'blood-
thirsty' I come by it legitimately. It's the only career
path open to me. Plus you should thank me! Being
kidnapped makes every white man a movie star. No

more paper pusher for you! You'll be a celebrity. You'll
be played in by the Toms Hanks or Cruise, or should
you die, a lesser star, unless you die heroically, and
then its one of the Toms again. Are there other dreams
than these?

EXUPÉRY: O a pirate! He's going to blow us all to kingdom come.

MUSE: That's right. Madness is my policy. It's mutually assured
destruction. I learned it from your centuree.

EXUPÉRY: Assange! Tunnel digger, money changer, your cult of
privacy gives aid and support to these evil doers. Muse,
do you have any idea what your piracy is doing to
insurance premiums?

[All others collapse in laughter]

MUSE: Sounds like highway robbery!

EXUPÉRY: *[Sulks]*

MUSE: Now you're sulking like a teen. If you keep this up, we'll
use your pipe to dig out your eyes and we won't let you
watch the second act. It will be highly educational, like
the first. And at the end there'll be a test. I'll give you
the questions in advance. Are you an 'environmentalist'
or just a 'mentalist'? Do you want these youth to chop
you up and feed you to fishies in their fishnets or will
you bend like a spoon?

OMNES DEAD YOUTH: Oh, we are bloodthirsty youth!

ASSANGE: If you don't mind, I don't care for all this violence.
It's very analogue
It's very twentieth cee.
It's not what I signed up for
when I signed up to go to sea.

Also, I must add that these youth are looking peaked
and less sexy by the day. Sweet siphons,
we must make our way for Magnetic Island soon.
We can picnic on Picnic Bay.

OMNES DEAD YOUTH: For I am tired mother and would fain lie doon!

ABDI WALI ABDULQADIR MUSE: for someone sour on the 20th c you're
a bit of a nostalgique.

ASSANGE: Too true.
I'm like Odysseus in that way
And every way. The very cleverest of boots.
That one skilled in the ways of contending.
Splendida mendax. But less bearded…
Anyway I'm just tired. Like the brochures say,
I need to reboot.
I need to relax, if lax I ever was.
I need a long layover at LAX
to spend time in an oxygen bar
And lay down in my oxygen tent
And think about my brood
Why don't you captain for awhile, ABDI WALI
ABDULQADIR MUSE.

[He lies down to sleep, as do DEAD YOUTH.]

MUSE: Very well then, intermission.

ACT THREE. PROLOGUE

[PROLOGUE appears. She is exactly as before. Except she has withdrawn her favor.]

PROLOGUE:
The SMIRK is groaning like a leaky kettle
like a laptop rank with STD's that cannot cool itself
its fan huffing, its motherboard melting
its hair limp,
like a lymphomic teen in hospice
on the death rattle. Hummmm. It's drowning
as it's droning. It's seeping slow cargo.
It drains. It sings a hott sonnette,
a sonatina. It terre hautes. BUZZ.
But is it day or night?
Does the firmament move?
I have the curiosity of a scientist.
I have the curiosity of a 1950's clinician.
But I have no mercy.
Nothing can exhaust me,
but nothing can feel what I feel.
I am become immortal,
and I have withdrawn my favor.

O SUSPENSION!
O grace withdrawn!
Ask the trilobite, he knows
what it's like to be suspended in media
To have the knowledge of centuries and no freedom
The prairie used to be a sea
but now its bed
is blocked in upright limestone
and has to supervise the foodcourt at the
Coral Ridge Mall
in Coralville, Iowa
shift after shift
it has to tolerate AC forever

Or hold up the Old Capitol walls
overseeing the 4H speech competition
drone drone forever and can never clock out
and can never sleep
and is suffered no Ambien.
Poor trilobite. You have suffered a sea change!
Immortalitee makes you fitful
it makes you petty as a queen.
I will not move this vessel
until its inmates find a way of moving me.
Act Three.

ACT THREE

[Dawn's Early Light. It is literally sickening, nauseous, unwell. DEAD YOUTH rouses itself]

DEAD YOUTH 1: Is it dawn? Or still night? O Christ it smells like a hospital gown

DEAD YOUTH 2: Hey presto, everything's going green. It's like the lockerroom at Greenpeace.

DEAD YOUTH 1: It's like something from a pamphlet at an STD clinic in a movie on TV.

DEAD YOUTH 2: "Sweet youth's temple, defiled!" Or misfiled, maybe. Misfired? Fumbled its missile sheild? Oh, damn the torpedoes!

DEAD YOUTH 1: Still, it stinks. Nausea gets its name from the sea.

DEAD YOUTH 2: So does the Seahag. Plus, we're in a total doldrum. We ain't goin nowhere!

DEAD YOUTH 1: This boat's got no motivation. It's got no inclination. It just sits and rocks.

DEAD YOUTH 2 : It's like those pamphlets they give you at juvie.

DEAD YOUTH 1: It's like those pamphlets they give you at the job center

DEAD YOUTH 2: Tips for going nowhere, for DEAD YOUTH.

DEAD YOUTH 1: Could it be we're in one of those useful Shakespearean mists, perhaps brought on by too much beauty cream on our eyelids or a frozen knock-off laptop screen or a tremor in the laser that reads the disk? Moments like these, which appear stagnant, are infact rich as cream, because a bug can enter the soup of plot and curdle the whole tureen. In the same way black energy moves in dark matter. Empty space can still conduct a field. An asp can emerge from aspic and scramble the mold! Then the gelatin flowers died for nothing. I mean the horse's crumply soles... Moments like these are in fact quiveringly equivocal bottoms for plot's top.

DEAD YOUTH 2: Ooh, you're so dirty with your bodily functions and horse hooves: "Give me a liver, a grille and a place to stand and I will eat the world." Well, who'm I kidding. I'm half rotten already. I'm ready to be upset. I'm a dead teen hockey team manager, for god's sake, not a veal calf. If I wanted safety, I wouldn't have spent all those evenings sneaking out to the parking lot behind the Jiffy Lube to meet grown men.

DEAD YOUTH 1: I'm always impressed by the sordidness of that story. It carries its bad outcome in its mouth. It's like a gleam where a pirate holds his knife between his teeth as he mounts the boat in silent moonlight on a painted sea in a picture book for kids, not even teens. Torn shirt and breaches. It leaves me breathless.

DEAD YOUTH 2: Well, me too, ultimately. Tell me this: have you got the itches? Do you find this nylon's starting to chafe?

DEAD YOUTH 1: I do. My scalp feels like a wig. My skin's going raw in places. There's nothing to eat on this boat. If I don't get some defragmentation soon and Big Gulp of sweet tea I'm not sure what's going to what.

DEAD YOUTH 2: Oh, why are we on this boat at all! You, me, the rest of the DEAD YOUTH, Mama JULIAN, ABDI WALI ABDULQADIR MUSE?

DEAD YOUTH 1: We're the rejects, the rejectimenta. Though its not true that we aren't somehow necessary for world's preferred plot to function, there has to be some cannon fodder, some credit card malfunction, some junk DNA, some user error, there has to be some losers, statistically, "success is counted dearest / to those who ne'er succeed," or else Utopia would arrive and stop the clocks forever, that's called evil. Evil decadence, evil pause. Arcadia Dance Party all ages but underage's the best... Mama Julian's just gathered us all up using some kind of juju algorithm or fishtank dipper-net. He's snipped the exterior links and resutured us. He's removed us from the plot.

[Large Thunderclap or Kaboom]

DEAD YOUTH 2: Sound like the plot wants us back!

DEAD YOUTH 1: I think it wants its ship.

[Thunder and lightening / Kaboom and flares]

DEAD YOUTH 2: Maybe they want the containers. Or the shit that's in the containers.

DEAD YOUTH 1: Mama Julian says its hundreds of metric tonnes of flip flops, slides and shower shoes. To be worn in worker dorms, assembly lines and correctional facilities. They serve as casual indoor shoes for all interior weathers and make it harder to run. But who would want to? And where to run to? O what to wear when you run when you have to to wherever you have to? But you know, at the factory where I worked making iPhones, they had to build a wall around the facility to keep jobseekers out! Of course it didn't work. That's human nature. It's also human nature to confess. A confession's a form of boast: unbecoming. That's what Mama Julian says. Anyway, they couldn't keep me out. I wouldn't tow the line. Well, I didn't actually work on the line. Instead I ran a, well, a concierge service, running numbers and a, you could say a matchmaking service. Until a big dog collared me and ran me out.

DEAD YOUTH: *[PROLOGUE steps on to the stage to help sing this]*
        That's human nature.
        Every part of this story.
        Part and parcel and particle collider and plastic
        carrier bag and shreds of particulates that turn the sea
        to slurry and lodge in the albatross guts
        bringing permanent curse on the shipping container
        making is stop in its tracks
        And from that toxic non-biodegradable preservative
        also rises a fume
        which is a human face
        which only has eyes for historee.
        Historee is porn for humans.
        A mise-en-abyme, a dummy company
        a self-programming story written by victors.
        It always gets the main points right.
        A thousand points of light!
        It gets right to the point.
        To knifepoint, gunpoint.
        To lablight and pornlight.

        [Thunder and lighting]
        The world is such a bad mother.
        [ramming and screaming]
        The world is such a bad mother.
        [retching and reeling]
        The world is such a bad mother.
        [shocking and squealing]
        The world is such a bad mother.
        [factory collapse]
        The world is such a bad mother.
        [factory collapse and coverup]
        The world is such a bad mother.
        [factory collapse and coverup and videoleak and crackdown]
        [and factory collapse]
        [A litter begins falling from the sky: dead technology.
        PROLOGUE smiles tightly, then exits.]

DEAD YOUTH, squealing:
Eek! content!

[Dead packaging. Dead devices. For example: dead monitors, dead keyboards, dead external disk drives, dead 'car phones,' dead memory cards, thumb drives, clam shells, walkmen, dvds, vhs, cds, wires, airphones, head phones, walky talkies, ceebees, two way radio devices. Possibly also dead seabirds. When the deluge has subsided to a light patter Julian ASSANGE rushes in and begins to dig his boys free from the rubble. They all sit atop the heap, visually data mining it and combing it and mentally organizing it into the useful and unuseful to the youthful.]

EXUPÉRY: *[walks on stiffly wrapped in kimono of plastic wrap and softly glittering fiber-optic tubing. She looks quite radiant. Softly.]*

DEAD YOUTH!

[ASSANGE goes on sorting through his heaps of recycling. DEAD YOUTH cocks up its head.]

DEAD YOUTH: What?

EXUPÉRY: Do you notice something different about me today?

DEAD YOUTH: You got free of the chair!

EXUPÉRY: Yes, I was able to undo the outerlayer. You're not so clever with analog knots as you are with encryption, tots.

DEAD YOUTH: Not so. My life was one continuous not. I lived in the abstruseness of that non-rational form. It's inspired all my subsequent non-choices. You see, I avoid all binaries *[dreamily]*... I do no programming at all. I'm what you call an end-user...

EXUPÉRY: Yes yes, of course, of course. Well, do you notice anything
       different cherubs?

DEAD YOUTH: You're upright.

EXUPEREY: Yes, we've covered that. It is this: my form's improved.
       I am streamlined.
       There is something about this swaddling in plastic that
       has caused my lines to align.
       It's a youthful predicament in which I find myself again.
       Immobilized in youth again at last at last.

DEAD YOUTH 1: Is it possible? Is it some trick? Perhaps the medical
       tube we utilized was rife with some bacterial slick and
       now it's playing a mad prank with his skin

DEAD YOUTH 2: Or with his mind. They say the skin of those
       asphyxiated with carbon monox is quite pink and quite
       smooth. I believe we have a stifler here among the
       DEAD YOUTH—we could ask him.

DEAD YOUTH 1: O Jeeze someone who passed on with his girlfriend
       listening to 'suicide solution'? Oh por favor! Plus who
       can afford a car anymore or that kind of suburban
       decline. But I do think we have a scarfer or two in the
       pack…some erotically curious pullet who clocked out
       in his closet in the banlieu…

DEAD YOUTH 2: Let's not squabble. This trussed up turkey's just a
       little hot from all that cellophane. He's got a bit high on
       his own fumes and now he's trying to divide and conquer.
       Shall we be conquered by a bake-sale goodie, a saran
       wrapped monster?

EXUPÉRY: Charming youth. I am an officer of the law, however
       compromised. To protect and serve is my infinitive and
       objectless charge. Now allow me to alert you to your
       true predicament. I sense you feel some loyalty to this

Assange. He's famous, or infamous, his hair is nice, he's
shown some interest in you, sunk his motherly claws in
you, lured or otherwise transported you onto this boat
which I admit must have seemed an impressive vessel to
such gutter trash as you I mean such innocents as you.

DEAD YOUTH 2: That's a laugh. Nobody's called me innocent before.
I was born in a carafe of legal guilt, free of compunction,
that's my element, my paradoxical alembic. I was so
adroit, a pick in a hot pocket. I came pre-programmed
for future crime...

EXUPÉRY: Enough navel gazing. My god. There's enough self-
regard on this boat to power the whole fleet. Boys, what
I'm trying to tell you is that time is running out. These
communication devices dropped here on the float by the
US NAVY. They want to lure Assange into some kind
of negotiation. Then when he's high on raconteurism
and decision trees they're going to swoop in and nab
the lot of you.

DEAD YOUTH 2: Really, this pile of junk?

DEAD YOUTH 1: It is an interesting pile. I was a bit tinkery in my
day. Model trains, stripped wires, shrapnel, pressure
cookers, there's a lot of very interesting trash here. In
general trash is more interesting and has more potential
than most are willing to admit. Of course that poten-
tial is a bit occult. Why look at our friend Muse, here!
Didn't he build himself a career from nothing. Just like
Mama Julian.

EXUPÉRY: And just where is this ABDI WALI ABDULQADIR
MUSE? You just met him. Your link to him is even
more tenuous than that of you to Assange. Look, free
me, I'll get you out of this mess. We'll signal the troops
with the glare of this cellophane and be lifted out of
here together.

DEAD YOUTH: *[raucously but rhythmically. They 'explode' in laughter]*
> HA !
> HA !
> HA !
> HA !
> We mean no offence, mon officeur.
> It's just that boys like me have heard every offer
> Dame Lubriciousness has on offer!
> We've been fit up for every frame-up, every ruse!
> But we refuse and refuse. We're refuse!
> HA!
> HA!
> HA!
> HA!
> Carnality, duplicity, depravity, calumny, rapacity,
> these are our fairy godmothers
> our lingua fracas! our sucre! our lucre!
> Our Ladies of the Perpetual Succor!
> HA!
> HA!
> HA!
> HA!
> For small change you could bend us over!
> For a snort you could sell us the bridge!
> But for nothing honey I won't arch my eyebrow, let
> alone my back!
> HA!
> HA!
> HA!
> HA!
> Do you think we're some holy innocents,
> like those dopes on the Children's Crusade?
> O livery! Sold into slivery?
> O knavery! Sold into slavery?
> Eli Eli lama sabachthani?
> HA!
> HA!
> HA!

HA!
O you may be the greasiest but hardly the slickest
pair of balls that tried to board this youth navy!

Ah! Hmm! *[they dry their eyes happily].*
Why don't you sit there and bake for awhile.
[they put a wad of cash in her mouth].

ASSANGE: *[he has been watching]*
            Children, that was magnificent.
            O you are loyal beasts.
            Perhaps because I fed you for so long
            from my own hand the red red meat.
            I mixed my own sweat with your feed
            The schwarma, the taco, the bolognees
            So that you wouldn't sting me, and, beelettes,
            you've been true!
            Dead youth, I have seen you admiring
            this throne of trash on which I sit.
            I don't know whether some convection current
            sucked it off the rank coast and threw it up here
            or if it's just some fetid militaristic gambit...
            The justice system can be pettier than a two-bit whore.
            It wants our welsh for its rarebit.
            It's disturbing. You would have to be a very sick fuck
            to shower children with toxic tech-waste and dead
            ocean fowls
            though what a fitting emblem of anthropocene
            moral principles!
            The self-congratulation of a decrepit species.
            I should embroider it on tea towels
            so we can contemplate it daily... As you can see,
            There's some exploded albatrosses here
            among the wires and motherboards—
            plastic corroded their stomachs and burst them as
            they began to decompose.
            A dead bird is maybe good for nothing but
            thinking about.

That's omenology. It made the Greeks wild.
Yet, are we better than the Greeks?
Thought is what we're all about!
And just now, I'm thinking, we have to get off this ship.
You fellows need to port up to the cloud
Rest, play, receive nutriment.
I need to redraw the plan.
My internal maternal gland tells me we are not far from
Magnetic Island.
But how will we get there if the ship won't move?
O if only Cook's miracle could perform itself again
When his compass needle began to dance according to
some magick
pointing him to Magnetic's shoaly shoals..
If only some comparably rogue magnetization
could reanimate these carcasses of computers
or get these dead birds to sing
and yield the secrets still programmed in their muscle
memory
communicate the route
And make this ship to move!

*[YES. THIS IS WHAT HAPPENS. A ROGUE
MAGNETIC CURRENT, THE SAME WHICH
DERANGED COOK'S COMPASS NEEDLE IN 1770
electrifies and reanimates the ship-board refuse. Dancers
made of decomposed birds and junked electrical equipment get
to their feet. They begin to perform a dance which is utterly
inhuman and involves pointing with beak or wing the direction
to Magnetic Island. The dance might be reminiscent of the
dance of the Morrigan on the batlefields of Ulster. Also the
same principle of plural bodies as pertains to the Morrigan.
Google this. As they perform this dance they make the
noises which resemble the three names of Magnetic Island:
Magnetic Island, Maggie Isle, and Yunbenun, emerge from
around the stage in would Shakespeare would call a 'dispersed
burden'—a burden in everyone's mouth. Eventually the
sound organizes itself into a song. The cash may even be*

removed from Exupéry's mouth so that he may participate in
the conjuration. At some point in the center of the configuration
should emerge MUSE. MUSE'S dance should be smooth,
strong, frank, and almost rhetorical. He is more concentrated
and more charismatic than any of the other figures on the stage.
His intelligence turns inwards and outwards at the same time.
He is an impossible circuit. He is a building and dispersing field.
The birds frame him. His dance is legible. He is form itself. He
is the form the human brain is ready to perceive. He is thus the
most human. He may dance with his gun.]

Magnetic Island
Yunbenun
Maggie Isle

Magnetic Island
Yunbenun
Maggie Isle

Esperanto
Smart Phone
Green Banker
Microchip
Paraben
Microloan

Magnetic Island
Yunbenun
Maggie Isle

Magnetic Island
Yunbenun
Maggie Isle

Coca cola
coca cola
Coca cola
Motorola

War on Terror
Andy Warhol

Magnetic Island
Yunbenun
Maggie Isle

Magnetic Island
Yunbenun
Maggie Isle

Zombie music
Therapeutic
Cash infusion
Vaccine Program
Carabinieri
World Bank

Magnetic Island
Yunbenun
Maggie Isle

Magnetic Island
Yunbenun
Maggie Isle

Austerity's
mysterium
Delirium's
Magisterium
Disappearing
notional wealth

combat diamond, combat metal,
combat water, combat home
combat jacket, combat trauma
combat pay, combat training
combat rape, combat breathing

combat stance and payday loan

Magnetic Island
Yunbenun
Maggie Isle

Magnetic Island
Yunbenun
Maggie Isle

Adar Abdurahman Hassan
Christine Assange
wiabu
Shahidika
Reshma
Tramelle Sturges
desaperacida
desaperacida
desaperacida *[repeat until unbearable]*

Magnetic Island
Yunbenun
Maggie Isle

Magnetic Island
Yunbenun
Maggie Isle

[Silence.]

PROLOGUE: *[walking on]* I am propitiated. I propagate
my malicious line.

ASSANGE: We move!

ACT FOUR: Magnetic Island!

*[A diagram. An engraving. One side of the stage is lit with
a hazy sunny humid light. One side of the stage has an
interrogation lighting, perhaps some realist chairs and
tables. Sun on one side, moon on the other. The division is
a bit Platonic, a bit Exupéry, a bit Elizabethan masque.
Stage makeup is thick on Assange and crew. They have been
translated into beings of Art. At the center, with a foot in
either orbit, stands MUSE. EXUPÉRY, in a cape of trash
but wearing his swart kepi and stage makeup, including a
pencil moustache, sits at the Interrogation desk. ASSANGE
and YOUTH are arranged in loving but troubled tableau in
the sunshine. For example: Four Saints in Three Acts]*

MUSE: Now, thanks to a late issue
    of slick, malignant cells from unknown sources,
    we have slid across the very ocean.
    We have arrived at Magnetic Island.
    An allegorical masque. A dome of pure thinking.
    As you will note, I hold the center of the stage.
    I drink the light through my skin like black narcissus.
    Dahlia Noir,
    my stage name. Mama Julian here is La Dame Aux
    Camilles.
    AKA Camille Le Blanc as in J'ai pas sommeil. We
    shared that role
    as juvenile performers.
    "O mon sommelier, I cannot sleep with this CUT
    THROAT!"
    How we tripped the boards in our peekaboo trousers
    on our pieds noir….
    But now we've run through our youthful qualities.
    It's time for my soliloquy.

    [Clears throat]

    According to Mother, I was just a teen like any teen

when I left Gyalko, just two weeks back
with nothing but the nylon jacket on my back.
Did I have time to become noble? To learn a role?
No. I have just as much sex drive, idealism, hunger and
violence as any other teenager of God.
Statistically average in terms of chemical composition.
I come from a part of the world where the maps
tore through
from too much loving rubbing with the eraser.
So edible, so pink...and with a pinky fume...
Something there is that doesn't love a map, like war
butter and treasure. Europe held us to its bosom like
a drunk mother
till it didn't. Then it became a drunk uncle,
poking us under the tarp.
But no matter. But more matter, more Art.
The mighty Ulster warrior Cuchullain
tied himself with his own innards to a standing stone
that his enemies might not realize he was dead
nor his friends either and end the war too soon.
And so I beat on. Language is my cinch and noose.

I should have died in the womb.
of malnutrition or machete by the age of three
But my mother tended me
But my mother died for me by refusing to die.
By coding me with the
REFUSAL TO DIE. So I refuse to be your tragic youth,
what your machine needs to blow off steam
in a whistle or a shriek.
The file it deletes as it performs its system
maintenance
its statistical depredations. NO.
Apparently I wrote a note
inside that boat, in the blood that flew
from my own tender throat. And I blamed it all
on foreign wars.
No, that wasn't me. Apparently I was a little handsy

when we hooked up in my dorm room No.
I did not attend UMass Dartmouth
failing every subject but creative writing. No.
But I did kill my mother who bought me the guns
to make the peace between us
before I left for the school. I columbined.
Sic semper tyrannis.
I did meet my murderers in a bar. I knew them from
high school.
Nope. I was a Red Guard, bayonetting books
until the day I thought to open one,
then took the poison whole
in sick bay til I could not longer hold the bayonette.
NO. DON'T BARK.
SPEAK THE LANGUAGE OF THE SPANISH
EMPIRE!
wasn't me. Act gratuit
wasn't me. Run the gamut
wasn't me. Instagram'd the gang rape
nope. Tied a cash register to Emmett Till's chest
with barb wire and riverrunned him
no. Destroyed the village to save it
no. 3/5ths compromise wasn't me.
9/11 wasn't me. Operation Enduring Freedom
wasn't me. Allah, allah, allah, allah.
Regime change wasn't me.
Credit default swaps wasn't me.
I was 16. I didn't have a chance to come into my
full criminalitee.

Upon a peak at Darien
Upon a peak at Darien
Upon a peak at Darien
Darien Darien
Smallpox blanket
Colonie collapse or
colonie
wasn't me

Motives are bunk.
Motives are for movies
Motives serve the plot.
But I serve nothing
except Allah. And only there
as befits an ambivalent teen.
Motives are a term of tee vee law
part of a holy trinittee.
Means, motives, or opportunity.
When did I ever have means
when did I ever have opportunities
and since I respectfully refuse to take up your 'motives'
except panic, hormones, and a light desire to eat—
that makes me a zero a cipher
a zed a nothing in your programming
a hitch a zilch a full stop
that makes the code stutter
that dithyrambs the logarithm
and calls off the search.
The search engine stalls out like the SS Smirk.
If I must have a mask
let it be zero. Otherwize
I won't participate in tragedee.
Motives are to me
what grappling hooks are to
deep sea divers. Throw me an anvil
and teach me to fish forever.
I'll lie under the sea, fishing, fishing,
and lying, lying. *[strapping on his 'zero' mask]*
Now I'm invisible
now I'm a green screen
the weather crawls
on top of me
And these are the pearls
that were my eyes...

*[Climbs up on a box like Abu Ghraib, statue of liberty,
Mother Erzulie, etc.… Company may decide its associations]*

DEAD YOUTH 1: What is it Christmas already? Is Muse the
Christmas tree?

DEAD YOUTH 2: Or a cell phone tower? Or Ariel in the Tree?

DEAD YOUTH 1: Turn him like a weathervane. See if our reception
improves.

JULIAN ASSANGE: Enough. I don't like all this poking at dear Muse.
I don't like all this prodding. For all we know, he's the
magic ingredient
that allowed our capsule to break down in the gut of
plot so perfectly.
To arrive at Magnetic Island.

DEAD YOUTH 1: O this island. It's a pit.

DEAD YOUTH 2: It's a dump.

DEAD YOUTH 1: It's a mass grave!

DEAD YOUTH 2: Without the masses. It's deserted.

ASSANGE: Not at all. It's just the off-season. You boys play the
part of the unseasonable youth. Untimely plucked. Watch
out or you'll be juiced. *[his tail switches like a lazy cat]*

EXUPÉRY: *[from office area]* ABDI WALI ABDULQADIR MUSE

MUSE: I recognize the representative of France.

EXUPÉRY: You are not the judge!
Nor president pro temp!
You do not recognize me.
I myself am JUSTICE.
I recognize you.

YOUTH TO YOUTH: HUM, blind justice recognizes muse!

YOUTH TO YOUTH: That's what, in science, we call a double-blind.

TOUT YOUTH: A very pharmaceutical pursuit! Forsooth.

EXUPÉRY: Silence, youth! It is golden.
    It has a mouth, but it's fixed.
    Like a clock, or a neutered cat,
    or suit brought against an emperor.
    In other words, can it.

YOUTH: Silence in other words! That is strange science!

EXUPÉRY: Let the interrogation proceed. Now, Muse, I don't want
    to have to take out my carburetor or my salad tongs. So
    answer my questions. Sing, muse.

MUSE: I wont.

EXUPÉRY: Then prattle.

MUSE. The only emperor is the emperor of ice cream.

YOUTH: The only emperor is the emperor de glace

MUSE the only emperor is the one who stands naked

YOUTH: the only emperor is the emperor sans pants

MUSE And communicates to youth, directly in his nakedness

ASSANGE: O dream of a crystalline communication.
    Flap flap to dirty ears. The pidgins of pigeons.
    The germs they smuggle in their penates and pinions.
    The germs they share for a puddle of crumb-ions.
    Good pigeons, grey matter, rats with aspirations!
    O rank mass, its rank communicants! Its holy
    communications!

YOUTH: We Catholics believe in transubstantiation.
        Our uncanny valley runs on circuits of revulsion.

MUSE: How like a thing, how like a paragon

YOUTH: how like a think, how like an epicure

MOUSE: how like a stink, how like a pedicure

YOUTH: how like bacteria that thrives in the footbath

MUSE: how like a strand of flesh-eating staph

YOUTH: how like the society ladies hobble on no feet

MUSE: until they realize it makes their jimmy choos fit better
        to have no feet

YOUTH: how they then occupy the lotus position

MUSE. how like a bath salt

YOUTH: how like a bidet

MUSE: What a piece of… work is man

YOUTH: this line should be 'le seul empereur est l'empereur de
        la crème glacée'

MUSE : Caveat emptor

YOUTH : Lasciate ogne speranza, voi ch'intrat

MUSE: Follow your leader. That's called dictee.

EXUPÉRY: I see you are a very learned man.

MUSE: Maleducated. Malaparte. That's why we formed our bande

à part. Before the Little Emperor could pursue his
destiny, he flipped the 'Malaparte' to 'Bonaparte.' A
visionary must also have a literalist's heart. And wear it
like a medal on his chest.

EXUPÉRY: O what a fine speech! O medals all around!

YOUTH: *[affixing metals by driving pins into Muse's torso. He now
resembles a Sebastian]* That's tantalum, that's for capacity,
in hearing aids, jet blades, and telephony. There's
cassiterite that's for circuitboards. And there's wolframite
that's for 'green ammunition', i.e. bullets with less lead.
So children who eat bullets won't get lead poisoning
and perform poorly in standardized tests. Also good for
making your iPhone vibrate.

ALL: What?

YOUTH: I kid you not. Wolframite is a very right metal. People
mine each other for it. I'm talking about a combat mine,
mined by gangpresed soldiers. I am not even talking
about a data mine.

ASSANGE: OH MUSE you are a bouquet. You are a very directory,
a very index, the very body of contemporary miseree.

EXUPÉRY: That's enough. Don't encourage his vanitee. Second
question. MUSE, when brought to trial in New York,
why did you smile for the cameras.

MUSE: Because I have a face.

[rimshot]
[rifle crack]

EXUPÉRY: WHAT'S THAT?

MUSE: Because I have a face.

EXUPÉRY: OBSCENE ANSWER!

MUSE: It is the opposite of obscene. The obscene must be
hidden from view. My face I show. It is a black face, but it
is not in blackface. It comes from a black site. It is a leak.

EXUPÉRY: Oh Obscene. O how his teeth gleams, his smile, and his
eyes, his charisma, and his native talent for being alive. O
obscenity. What a felony! Youth tar him with petroleum
products. Then he will know what it means to be in
capitalism's embrace. IN THE BOSOM OF THE LAW.

YOUTH: *[tar Exupéry instead]*

EXUPÉRY: WHAT? What is the meaning of this?

YOUTH: Are you not the font of Justice? I recognize you, I met you
so many time on the other side of the bench. You sent
me to juvie for a decade, took the kickback to buy golf
clubs. Luckily I OD'd and was thus released from my
sentence, albeit to the morgue. Now you wear black
robes you wore in life, which shows you have been
invested with gravure, as in the grave.

EXUPÉRY: Well I see. Grandeur is grand. That's tautologee, a
very right and total logic. Let us proceed with the
proceedings. Where were we?

MUSE: You asked me why I smiled, and I replied, because I have
a face.

EXUPÉRY: Yes, yes. And yet the next day, at your trial, you wept and
wept. Why did you weep?

MUSE: Because I am a teen. Because I had just learned the role cut
out for me. The role of tragic youth. I didn't want it,
but could not avoid it. I was trapped. And I wept because
I had tears at my disposal. And I disposed of them. Or

perhaps I had a grit in my eye. Perhaps I thought I could weep out an industrial diamond so tough I could use it as a weapon and cut up the court.

EXUPÉRY: O, a threat! A threat against the body of the court. Oh what a mongrel! And yet we cannot lose our composure. As a final piece of evidence, I would like to read out something you wrote on your blog. "I think I should select from my poems as my favorite the Emperor of Ice Cream. This wears a deliberately commonplace costume, and yet seems to me to contain something of the essential gaudiness of poetry; that is the reason why I like it."

MUSE: I wrote that?

EXUPÉRY: Yes, rat and you are trapt. You are trapt forever in your own snare because you wrote this on the Internet. It's data. It's datestamped.

MUSE: When did I write that?

EXUPÉRY: You wrote in 1933 in Hartford Connecticut.

MUSE: Well then I denounce it. That was in my youth. Before I came into my revolutionary consciousness. Emperors indeed. Though the essential gaudiness of poetry is quite a phrase, something to hold on to, to pin to the breast…

EXUPÉRY: Your opinion about emperors has no bearing on this case. My god, you blacks. Whine whine. Somalia hasn't been ruled by an emperor for at least…well, decades. As for ice cream, typically childish. I can't understand this substance's resurgence in this play as a motif. I thought this was a play about petroleum.

DEAD YOUTH: Judge, if it please the court, I'd like to file a brief. Ice

cream and petroleum are polar opposites of each other,
and thus may substitute for each other, bind, and form
a digital system. We pow'r this colony with the swerve,
with the flip-flip. Then we can parade about in Speedos
and flip-flops, and have ice-cream in the freezer and
run the vaccuum cleen all night. As for me, like a true
hustler, I like both oil AND ice cream. I'm ecumenical.
Look, I've black nylons under my track bottoms. My
jacket's so synthetic it could melt.

EXUPÉRY: Silence, dead pageboys. You call that trash philosophie
the 'idealism of youth'? With that kind of idealism you're
more suited for a Weimar cabaretto than the Furor's
youth. Now, like the Furor, let's be rational and logical.
Let's review the facts of the case. Your excuse for your
great crime of piracy is your youth. An excuse immedi-
ately invalidated by the fact that you are being tried as an
adult. Therefore, ipso facto, you are no youth, therefore
you are defenseless. You sir, are no youth! QED. GED.
JD. STD. Associates Degree from the Lice Lycee. Also,
since you refuse to ascribe to yourself a motive, I must
assign one to you, and I shall select one that is more than
mere larceny, which would be par de course. No, sir, let
me see....your motive is villainy, villainy itself, tout court
and tout suite, and your wish to see villainy communi-
cated to the innocent flank of the world, in the person of
the MV Maersk which you so wantonly call 'the Smirk.'
O piracy! O cult of villainy! O cur! O scourge! O stur-
geon with black eggs! O rub his face in shoe polish, shoe
'blacking' burnt corn cobs and ash! I should sentence
you to DEATH. O, but being Just I love MERCY. So
instead I shall transport you to Terre Haute Indiana for
thirty-three-and-one-third years. Don't snuffle you'll
emerge an exhausted 51. Though I dare say you'll have
lost your looks.

YOUTH: No, MUSE, we will not let you perish! You or your good
looks! You are a role model to us!

MUSE: DEAD YOUTH, I am not a role model. I'm not even an
           athlete. My only mission is not to die before my time. I
           wanted to say my piece, and my piece is over. And yet, I
           feel a tear forming right here. In these two organs which
           are to sight what hearing is to ears. I mean my eyes.
           They're pearlescing. They're dropping white bacterial
           wads in front of me. O I lose my vision. I am become a
           twin of justice. I am a white world. I am blind.

YOUTH: No! There is one more hope! A deus ex machina! A
           pederastic stroke of plot's ass by the divine.

[they gather around Muse like women at the tomb of christ]

ASSANGE: I believe it is time to reveal myself.
           No, I do not claim to be the son of the Divine
           I think I'm a little smarter than him
           I'm not going to do the eli eli lama sabachthani
           just because some moron spills the salt
           or tears up when the cock cries out
           in some damp suburban hideout.
           If there's one error you can count on,
           it's human kind. I have been betrayed so many times!
           But I am the son of Christine Assange,
           who survived. In the Anthropocene,
           and at the mercy of men and their
           financial instruments, that is no small thing.
           People, a conspiracy is an engine.
           It is also a computer.
           A thinking machine.
           It can think better than any single component entity.
           this conspiracy. Another name is Wikileaks.
           I built Wikileaks to be the CIA of the people of earth
           so that they could know the workings of their own states
           in perfect Transparencee. The veil is rent! Or at
           least soilent.
           For this I have been reviled as some kind of reptile
           the Original Wriggler, the one with no conscience.

Who only loves his own blonde hair and fame.
I mean the odd snake who's gay and rapes women
you meet so frequently in films and not on earth.
Still, I won't entirely refute the charges
because I love films. Though I'm organic.
I come from a blonde.
Sometimes I think I'm a little John Lennon
with my idealism, and my disappearing acts,
and my feminine good looks, and my conspiracee.
He wore those granny glasses to bring the truth
to light.
But really, the truth was as plain as blacklight.
the truth was a black eye.
the truth was a bottle, blonder.
A blonde of gold and tungsten
A wiry blonde, a blonde of wiring
A nylon blonde, a blonde of laddering
A punched-out blonde, a blonde of hiding
A blonde of smuggling and a blonde of trafficking
I change my hair when I'm being followed
I've learned that from the movies
A blonde of dubiety and a blonde of beauty
two blonde suns would make the sky fall down
pull the universe apart with too much gravity
Everything's God's fault
because god is not a mother.
O Christ I'm an atheist I only believe in bad motives
and mothers
And in computers. Tho mothers can have bad motives
and bad mothers can have good motives and computers
can have no motives.
Something can be itself or its opposite.
Zero can be one. The value is not significant
but the difference is. When there is no difference,
that's where the digital collapses and gives birth to
the virtual.
That's where the virtual betrays the digital
and is a bad son.

I'm still toting this box
its full of bees but they might be dead
I don't know, it's Schrodinger's symbol
it's Turing's cervix
inside the box
actions are performed not as on a theater stage
where all the world is, merely players
and etcetera
no as in a black box
lost at cee when the plane went down
the chatlogs of catastrophe
a blacksite, a torture space
most profound
you have to share your cell with a dead cat
who might yet be alive
twitch twitch
bird brain

the virtual lives in the box
the virtual pours from the box

it's not that we don't know the facts
but that there might be no facts
quote unquote
the only place I feel safe is the Internet
quote unquote

I call that faith
which looks like fame
the drug the universe loves
I mean the Internet
eats and shits, makes more of
smears on everyone's face
I call myself St. Julian Assange
I am such a massive blonde
I should have my own SS
and I do: the SS Smirk...

and from the outside it looks like the universe
closed in on itself
brooding
but inside
but inside
but inside
but inside
but inside
but inside
but inside

it is a massive ride
it propagates massive fields
you can't ride there with your citizen self
you can't ride there with your Cartesian self
it cops a massive feel
so tiny and so mass mass doesn't mean mass anymore
a mass defection, a genuflection, a granule smaller than
a flea's ass could crash
the gala ball
the galaxy's confection
Henrietta Lacks

conspiracy is an engine
conspiracy is a machine
it thinks better than the individual human
but like anything built by humans
its faults are human faults
it is vulnerable to betrayal and confession
bad fits of conscience
given the bad behavior of the creator I believe
if there is a Divine man made it
it is a human product
and will have human problems
unless we can work around it
by not being humans
by being Divine, not alive
I have been a shit on earth

I will be in heaven, and on the Internet,
and in this box,
a beautiful thing
streaked in gold
I will move in the heavens like bad news
my own omenology
an encrypted key
a monstrance
a lock box
made available for public veneration
visible yet invisible
venereal like a golden chancre
God pins to the very cervix of his sanctissima
it will hold and expose all the leaks in the sea
and free all the capped-boys from their tethers
and buoys from their links

but for now *[takes out large scissors and begins to shear his hair to the scalp]*
we hide
in plain sight.
we form an engine
called conspiracy
[he dons a prison guard outfit, and so do the DEAD YOUTH]
and with this engine
we reanimate the dead carcass of this cul-de-sac
and steer it to our next paradox
[they fit an orange jump suit over muse, and lift him to the ground]
the federal correctional complex
most suited to a pirate
for his crimes against the see
is a very inward empire
with no externalitee
with no coastline
but the locks and high walls
of a paradox: a very landlocked port.
There he will be housed in the

Communications Management Unit
ie an incommunicado sound set
that looks like prison life
but is just for Muslims
and has no telephone, mail, visits or ISP
there he will turn his face from obscenity to obscurity
never to sully with his visage
what is so prized in Terre Haute:
Malls, landlines and shooting ranges.
And when he has become an ultradense
packet of information
we will release him back into the system
to explode it with his dark energy.

Gentlemen, to Terre Haute.

[they march Muse off as a police escorte]

*[the interrogation light becomes superbright on the
immobilized Exupéry and suddenly blacksout]*

EPILOGUE

PROLOGUE-AS-EPILOGUE

The play is over. I am still me.
I have transformed myself to Epilogue
also known as Epithelia
not known as Apologee.
The past is resourceful.
It does not wait.
It contaminates the future
with its DNA mistakes.
The past sails like a sinking ship
that does not sink, but leaks waste.
Till the bottom of the sea is barren.
And a dense mat of toxins o'er grows the earth
rank as a fridge after a hurricane.
The isle is full of dead fridges, going green.
There is no exit.
I sit at the lab bench and eat my lunch.
The lab is deserted. The scientist is dead
who first harvested my tumor
who sentenced me to immortality.
I who was only known for hospitality
to be re-writ as permanent malignancy.
I grow and I grow alone
in culture. I write code.
I distribute copies. I propagate my line.
Maybe I am QUEEN BEE
in my colonie. Maybe I am
QUEEN HACKER. Queen Julian Assange
because I make everything over
with my queer authoritee.
I change my hair when I am being followed
No. I cannot change my hair.
It always stays just like this
'dancing towards my face.'
I participated in this human drama

because the immortal must have their amusements
& because it makes a change.
& I cannot change
I must perform my toxic ministry forever.
I never go off-shift.
Julian Assange:
all secrets are the same secret.
The only secret is this:
The only emperor is malignancy.
That's human nature:
malignancy
atrocity
maliciousness
malevolence
violence
exploitation
abjection
laughable naiveté
and no expiration date
until the end of the Anthropocene
and after that, who knows?
I predict
my after-afterlife will be like this:
when the freezers run out of current
when the vials and petri dishes warm
when my cells in culture grow
without human hands to coaxe them
I'll find no relief
from immortality
but must always grow more of me
dead bell
dead bell
I ring for thee
the suffering, and the malignant
the greedy, and the helpless
the vulnerable, and the rich
the unfit and the fit
the guilty and the blameless

I am the mother of these
there is enough of me
for each of thee
I am unlimited credit
I am unlimited debt
I am the mother of this planet
I am forced to be
I am forced to be
yoked to thee
Anthropocene
Fate would not let me die with the twentieth cee
Now I myself am Fate; I ride the night bus
I travel on the maternal line
I arrive ahead of schedule. I speed time.
I clasp the future to my breast
like a Bible, a pearl-toothed baby or a pest
I let it sink its teeth in me
I let it lower its pipette
deep down to my malignant layer
and drink from me
until the future
looks like me
& acts like me
and is me
as I am forced to be
it with its brown hair
'dancing towards its face'
its skin light and smooth as a fawn's
its painted nails abide no chip
it rests slim fingers
on its woman's hips
this futurity
is a kind of divinity
it has a name like me.
Henrietta Lacks.

ACKNOWLEDGEMENTS

Loud thanks to the Cathy Hong and Danniel Schoonbeek of the PEN America website, to Joe Pan at Hyperallergic, and to David Blumenshine & crew at Similar Peaks for giving these fun-loving DEAD YOUTH an Internet home.

Even louder thanks to Fiona Templeton, E. Tracy Grinnell, and Caroline Bergvall for selecting this play to inaugurate the Leslie Scalapino Award, and to the admirable actors at The Relationship who dazzled me with the baller way they put on all this ornate language like a costume and swaggered around.

& gratitude to Leslie Scalapino, whose *Dahlia's Iris* first gave me the inkling that one character might serve as a medium for another, one body a medium for another, one genre a medium for another, and that the whole non-Cartesian assemblage could host improbably occult effects and propagate uncanny fields.

Freedom for Chelsea Manning, Julian Assange, and Abdi Wali Abdulqadir Muse. This play is a spell for their safety.

Peace and sweet dreams for the once and future DEAD YOUTH.

A NOTE ON SOURCES

I first learned of Henrietta Lacks, the Prologue and presiding deity of this play, from my colleague Steve Tomasula's *VAS: A Novel in Flatland.* My knowledge of Lacks was made more acute by Rebecca Skloot's *The Immortal Life of Henrietta Lacks.* I am indebted to Skloot's description of Lacks's iconic photograph— "She looks straight into the camera and smiles, hands on hips, dress suit neatly pressed, lips painted deep red"—for the opening image of my play, and also for the image of pearls which arises on page 11. Skloot describes Lacks's autopsy thus: "And her organs were so covered with white tumors it was as if someone had filled her with pearls." In the opening and closing lines of this play, the phrase in quotation marks paraphrases a remark by Lacks's cousin, Sadie Sturdivant, as quoted in Skloot's book. Sturdivant describes Lacks as wearing her hair "just like it was dancin toward her face."

OTHER WORKS BY JOYELLE McSWEENEY

The Necropastoral: Poetry, Media, Occults
(University of Michigan Poets on Poetry Series)

Percussion Grenade
(Fence Books)

Salamandrine, 8 Gothics
(Tarpaulin Sky Press)

Deformation Zone: On Translation
(Ugly Duckling Presse)

Flet
(Fence Books)

Nylund, the Sarcographer
(Tarpaulin Sky Press)

The Commandrine and Other Poems
(Fence Books)

The Red Bird
(Winner of the Fence Modern Prize; Fence Books)